Believing Their Shadows

Believing Their Shadows

Poems by Anne Colwell

Anne Colwell

Word Press

To Nancy —
With thanks for our long
friendship and for all your
encouragement and support!
Love,
Anne

Published by Word Press
P.O. Box 541106
Cincinnati, OH 45254-1106

ISBN: 9781936370030
LCCN: 2010933027

Poetry Editor: Kevin Walzer
Business Editor: Lori Jareo

Visit us on the web at www.word-press.com

Acknowledgements

"Adulteress" and "Mary Tells Her Side" first appeared in *The Writer's Room* (Ed. Eve Shelnutt). "Troop 603," "The Centaur Comes Down Main Street in March," and "Voice on a Train Out of Grand Central" first appeared in *Midwest Quarterly Review*. "Christina River" first appeared in *Southern Poetry Review*. "Field" appeared in *Small Pond*. "Vacation Picture" appeared in *Nightsun*. "Man with a Hammer" appeared in *Hedge Apple*. "Casida of an American Woman" and "Your Skin and How to Live In It" appeared in *Dominion Review*. "The Virgin and the Dynamo" appeared in *Eclectic Literary Forum*. "A Story I Have For Parties" appeared in the *Evansville Review*. "Casida of Waking" and "Casida of the Longed-For Lover Forlorn in the Airport" both appeared in *Phoebe*. "Casida of the Lover's Seasons" appeared in *California Quarterly*. "Casida of Bible Belt Radio" appeared in *Writer's Room*. "Hammerhead," "Cake," "Crickets" and "Processional" first appeared in *The Central California Poetry Journal*. "Funerals and Fairytales" appeared in *Poetry on the Page Magazine*. I am grateful to the Delaware State Arts Council for awarding me the Individual Artist's Fellowship.

Table of Contents

I. Look For Me At Noon

Ferry Ride

That weekend came in poems,
    in images that we,
both suffering the same compulsion,
    would set down,
so those days could never wriggle off
    the page, or get mislaid,
    but even so.
That dinner we made together, we ate.
    Smells of cumin, garlic, ginger mixed
    and dissipated through the open window.

On Sunday's ferry ride, we sat together
    among tourists— all home now—
who forced wriggling children to stand still
    and smile right— not that frozen grin!

On that ferry the life preservers
    hang everywhere and children pitch,
laughing, on unsteady legs.

At the end of that good weekend we sang
    "White Squall" to the tame swells of the bay.
I held your wrist hard
    felt the inexorable clock
    throb beneath your skin.
And I prayed
    to your wrist's beat
that if I say this right,
    force this wriggling child into the picture,
even with a frozen grin,
    we will know each other again
when that other ferry bumps to a stop,
    we will have this

even after we cross
the still river of forgetting.

Vacation Picture

Your hair is thin and dark, caught back in a scarf.
You're posing— 1940's cheesecake: bathing suit,
anklets, loafers, leaning back on a pole by the
        wharf.

Behind you the rented beach house, the mute
sky, scrub pine, all synchronized tones of gray.
One hand dangles sunglasses. You look out with
        the absolute

smile of your fifteenth year. The year before the day
your father lay hemorrhaging on the floor,
before you and your mother learned to pay

off the debt of manlessness, before rationing, the war,
before late night car rides, flasks, double dates, red
lipstick, and red flashing lights, before

white lace, suburbia, tranquilizers, hospital beds,
hidden bottles, open regrets. Somewhere near you a
        gull cries,
a sleepy laughing sound. Listen. Lift your head.

Lean back against the warm tarry wood. Close your eyes
and breathe easy, easy a moment, under the
        changing skies.

13

Christina River

Where the tree leans dead into the water
the current left silt, last autumn's
leaves. The season's first rain made the river
muddy, fat, like a woman
due in March, mumbling in its sleep.

Swallows chickadees,
and snakes come. The turtle,
asleep under flattened shadows
of water striders, feels the slow
blink of body in the current
and the fallen rain.

She will heft her stony back,
move on clawed, stump legs.

Water striders, born awake,
skate still, easy in the rippling—
believing their shadows, never
imagining how slender a thing it is
to walk on water.

Casida of the Lover Longing to Return

—Seville, Holy Week

I will, I will come back,
when feria, drunken,
stabbed by a thief,
lurches wild-eyed
through its last days,
when saints float like corks
through church doors
on a river of carnation,
when black hooves
tattoo your ears and German
motorcycles jackhammer
your eyes' black stones.

Look for me then,
ignored in cafes
where my countrymen
boast of beloved
Minnesota.
Look for me,
alone in a flowered
horse carriage
beneath a black mantilla.
Look for me at noon.
I will turn the corner
of the cathedral
wearing its shadow
across my face, a veil
against the heat.

Mary Tells Her Side

We could only find one room
in that whole dusty city
though we knew every street.
     So all of us lay
     stretched on the floor
     or propped between chairs
     in the darkness.
My back to the cool of the wall,
I lay on my cloak
with my hair wound soft
beneath my head.

Long after the others were sleeping
with their fitful cries and mumbles,
     I lay still and quiet
     and listened hard for his breathing.

I can't remember
him coming to me
or hearing him cross
the sleeping room.
     But I knew.
     I knew his touch.
And when his fingers
brushed my breasts
my nipples opened up like flowers,
     like purple spikes of hyacinth.

And all that night in that molasses dark
thick and sweet my hands burned
and my feet flamed
     and my hair, loose between us, became
     a woven crown of fire.

And all night in that dark he came
with the deep light and burning
that I had known,
that I had seen him inspire.
But after that night,
after that night I was ruined.
The old things were gone.
And I never was again
without the sound
of wings in my head,
without the ache
in my small, dark womb.
And after that I never could again,
I never did,
with any man.

Holding Back

Coming home from the orthodontist
mouth filled with tightness
not yet ache,
I sat beside my mother
who steered the green Dodge
through Pennsylvania autumn,
always stopping at the dairy store
on Route 5— homemade ice cream,
homemade sign.

Freezer cases lined the back.
Behind them, a girl, smeary blue
eye shadow, lank hair,
handed over dripping cones.
Every visit there we'd walk around back
where, in decrepit chicken coops, somebody
(Could it have been that girl?)
kept peacocks.

Fascinated by their exoticness,
we watched that cock and his hen
strut and peck in pine needles
and leaf trash at the edge
of the parking lot.
What nostalgia makes it always fall
and always my mother, sober,
delighted by the tail full of eyes,
the misplaced lovers.

The Centaur Comes Down Main Street in March

I rode a centaur down Main Street
on a March afternoon, past
Newark Newsstand and Rosa's Pizza,
the burnt out, abandoned Opera House.
I ran my hand across parking meters
like a picket fence and then leaned
forward to place that hand on his chest
and tangle the other in his damp curled hair.

Then he said words as real as stones
to be kicked along and all the delicate
women crumpled their bags
and lowered their eyes.
He said words as real as years
with separate families and far away,
when he rides off
where his world goes and I live
in some trailer park
off the Cleveland highway.
When, failing our bareback
ride into the sunset, when,
maybe we don't even write,
but just remember,
while waiting for the plumber
who never shows
or sleepless and staring from a window—
one soft March at noon
we rode down Main Street and I leaned
forward
to lick the tip of his ear,

with a hand pressed to his chest
and another tangled in the hair
at the base of his neck.

Man with a Hammer

Loss and being lost
dried my eyes to plaster.

I went out looking for a man with a hammer.
Plaster
                  like grandmom's plaster
                  kitchen saints, but coarser,

and I found him standing by the train tracks
near the river.
                  "I thought you would bring me a
                  bird, a white bird as offering."

I said, "I have a ring. I have a necklace that
we've worn for generations,
                  but I have nothing that lives and
                  nests, nothing that can fly."

He looked to where two tracks become one by
the bent horizon,
                  then turned back to me and
                  sighed. Wiping a red scarf across
                  his eyes,

he said, "Well come then," and I stepped into
the circle of his arm
                  and bent backward and he
                  turned the scarf into a hammer.

Shatter the bones of my face. Scream open
caves of my sockets.
                  A sound like a train or the ruckus
                  of air and wings

and from the holes where plaster eyes had
been
           twin cataracts of starlings
           explode into the sky.

Black starlings boiling, blown into the air like
soot,
           a pestilence. He walks off down
           the tracks

twisting and untwisting the red scarf, then
tying it around his neck.

Redoing the Sistine Chapel
(in jigsaw)

Spread out the pieces.
Turn them over.

Bits of God
everywhere, creation
of the world,
of Adam, of order
from chaos.

Find the edges.

Dimension appears.
Names of the prophets
like place cards
and all over
the kitchen table

sculpted torsos,
arms like sailor's rope,
angelic feet,
Adam's left butt cheek

waiting to be pieced
again.

II. Hauntings

Ghosts

You wanted stories like
"The Mysterious Chamber" or
"The Legend of the Enchanted Soldier."
        We wanted it to "mean something"
        when you saw the Alhambra.
So we read what Irving gave
of beheaded Albencerrajes,
        all thirty-six haunting
        the Patio de Los Leones,
voices murmuring through the dark,
clinking of something like jewelry
        or chains. Moorish Princesses
        locked in towers, their beauty hidden
and saved. Treasure under the seventh floor,
the Devil's domain of the Justice Gate.
        But, when we saw the ruin,
the leap was too great
even for nine-year-old imaginings.

Even when I picked out what might have been
a blood stain on the floor,
        told you to listen by the fountain for
        their voices,
        you were not convinced.
There was no mystery that you could see,
that I could either, tell the truth,
        except maybe the mystery of tourists,
        cameras and sensible shoes,
the shared drive to see,
to have a record of having seen:

the memory that might be brought back
by shapes posed near fountains or arches.

The shades never grow older, or go away,
        captured like the Princesses, or,
like the Albencerrajes,
        our day will be preserved in shadows,
stains,
when our voices are the legends
        of fountains,
when you can read all the stories yourself
and have gone beyond the meaning
        we give you and we look
        at the pictures
from when you were nine
and we took you to the Alhambra.

Writing in the Margins

Ten years ago we were illicit.
The story romantic, cryptic
inscriptions in books, Dairmuid
and Grania, Tristan and Isolde,
love without rent or insurance.
I used to think, writing in the margins,
someday you'd sit alone in dying light,
see my writing, remember me,
like those mythic women, almost possessed
then lost, beautiful forever.

Back then you wrote
"Now has our winter come/It has
come down," describing the snow
as "benediction" over our warm house,
strong coffee, late love.
You made a winter
where you believed
there'd never be one.

I look for you now
out the picture window of our rented house
on the fifth day of a January
we will live together.
It has come down, our winter now,
our snow, shoveled out,
benediction and curse.
Your car coughs like a colicky baby
in the drive. Come in, love,
together we can face
and flee
the tyrants,
the bills from Christmas,

the leftovers dinner,
our real lives.

Accounting

The moments I want back
are all alike, predictable in
their dramatic finality: a closed
door, the knowledge that I can count
all the times I speak to, kiss
touch anyone I love before the door—

of a room, or a house, or a heart— the door
slides shut. The particular one I look back
to tonight belongs to an elevator in
a hospital in Wilmington where I leaned close
to my father's ashy face for a kiss
goodbye. But, to clarify my sad account

with less dramatic detail, my father was in
       accounting
there. He was not admitted— or even close—
admittedly ill. We'd had lunch in the back
of Madeline's at a table far from the street door
and bar. We spoke of my friend enlisted in
the Army, my father's stint as a PFC, when he
       kissed

my mother goodbye and knew with that kiss
he would come home, would come back
so he could marry her. I was that close
to asking if he'd been happy, in love, when the
       door
of the kitchen creaked open, the waitress
       counting
change into her palm, broke in

on our conversation, said to him, "Good to see

31

you in
here, hon. She's a fine girl. You've got to bring
      her back
for dinner sometime." Then we walked out the
      door
into July sun, strangely cool, the first kiss
of an October he would never see. Later, I'd
      count
the days he'd live beyond on one hand. Close

the other into a fist. The white car at the
      corner, his clothes,
his ring finger circling absently, wandering in
the pattern on his tie— I can see every detail; I
      can count
the people we walked by coming back from
      lunch. Until the door
of the elevator opened and I stepped out and
      leaned back to kiss
the face I can't kiss again. Tonight, I want to
      shove my hand back

between the closing doors, throw off the count
      by one kiss,
before we step back in— to his silence, my life.

Revenge

My mother haunts my kitchen.
Well, her ghost, to be precise.
Not in graveclothes now, not skeletal.
Just rummaging. Looking like she looked
in life— bloated, drunk, matted hair,
cracked bloody lips,
attired in bathrobe and scuffs.
I hear her opening the cabinets.
I see her
— in my mind's eye, Horatio!—
standing spotlighted
by the open refrigerator,
peering at sickly sweat
on yesterday's vegetables,
something rotting in tinfoil.
I lay upstairs and listen.
What could be down there
she'd want?
What could call her back here
from the undiscovered country?
Not a few pots, all of her
estate I got,
or the trivet that says
Mi casa es su casa.
Finally I get up,
heart louder than the rattling
silverware, no sword
or cross.
I creep down the stairs,
flick the switch.
Light spills
over scarred cabinets,
dishes hunched in the drainer,

the kingdom of
silent appliances.
Remember.

Funerals and Fairy Tales

In Czechoslovakia, a steel mill worker stood on
an overturned crate and proclaimed, or
proclaimed again, "We hold these truths to be
self-evident." Here in an American December,
I stood in front of Macy's perfume counter and
wished this Christmas I could buy you a
present. The counter was a glass box with
gold-edged trim; bottles lay inside curved like
women. I remembered seven dwarfs
mourning around a jewel case like that, glass
sides and gold, lined with pillows, fat satin
pillows for the crow black hair and blood red
lips. You and I went to many funerals,
followed the obligatory hearse through iron
gates to Holy Angels or Saint Anne's, climbed
out of our Ford, walked to the plot, the ground
uneven, mean with frozen ruts. Or, after the
thaw, our spiked heels wobbled, sinking into
loose soil where something might grow.
Mourning always made you sober. But then,
like Snow White, you never stayed frightened
for long. The witch in any disguise, the most
perfunctory old rags, could make you drink.
No song, no small neat cottage, no dwarf love
could be as red as that apple, all rotted inside,
fermented. Until finally I walked from your
grave into the salt dry snow of December. The
family ate chicken together and were secretly
relieved. The world was instantly new the
moment you left it, hopeful for the first time
and irredeemably lost. In Romania, there will
be enough food for the winter; kerchiefed
women stand in meat lines grinning. The

gruesome dictator has been deposed. And
children, whom years of rationing have
deprived, who've weathered one after another
cruel eastern winter, have oranges, real oranges
for the first time, and not knowing the first
thing about the sweet pulp of the center, they
bite right through the bitter rind.

Your Skin and How To Live In It

You had no idea, did you, that the title
meant actual skin, that the doctor
explained dermatological dilemmas
for women, unlovely, or heavy, or

old and adrift on seas of cream and promise.
Desperate when you pressed that ten
into my hand, you needed answers
beyond the surface, a way to open

those too fragile lids to ordinary pink
dawns. Those longings had grown:
the desire to stretch out beneath the freckled
sweep from collar bone to collar bone,

to curl contented in the shadow of your
lower lip, to ride at ease on the blood tide
of your own dermis, at home in the arch
of your foot, and the singular, wide

expanse of your intelligent forehead.
The book cheerfully debunked myths
of cellulite and weight loss cream.
You put the change toward a fifth

of something apricot-honey colored and less
mysterious than the teasing title, *Your Skin
and How to Live In It*. You escaped,
emptied the earthly habitation, your own skin.

Hammerhead

Some voice inside him said
"Turn and look" and there was the fin.
He held the net still,
felt his feet in his boots,
felt the bay crawl around him.

Then he noticed the way
the blue triangle swayed
in the swells, rocking
without volition,
and he tugged
the curious stillness in.

In the shallows, children gathered,
buzzing to see,
touching the body with sticks.
Schools of tiny black fish
spilled over the white tongue
shining like starlings or summer flies.
But what amazed most
were the eyes, each eye
terribly alone on either side
of the bone buttress.

The fisherman took out pliers
and pulled at its teeth.
I wanted one for luck.
But each broke off, delicate
white shards in his hand.
He threw the body
back on the sand and waded
out again with his net.
Even the children tired of looking

finally. But for hours,
as word passed, casual couples,
walkers, sifted down the beach
for one last look
from each cold eye.

Meditations: Divine and Mortal

"You once desired me to leave something for
you in writing that you might look upon, when
you should see me no more; I could think of
nothing more fit for you nor of more ease to
myself than these short meditations following"
Anne Bradstreet to her son Simon in the
dedicatory letter to *Meditations: Divine and
Moral*, March 20, 1664

I think of Simon Bradstreet combing
Meditations for an explanation
that certainly isn't there
of an arched eyebrow, or the story
(told once, now hopelessly confused)
of some uncle's difficult horse,
the aunt who embroidered
the wedding dress.

Divine and Moral: she tried to give
all she knew, but it can't be enough.
Children never ask the right questions,
and, no matter what,
what's left behind suffers in translation.

Looking out the window, away
from her spinning, in the last place
she would live, if she thought
of her other houses burning,
thought to put something of her
own journey down for him,
it was more than most.
Though, of course, wholly inadequate.

When I was twelve or thirteen
I found an old tape recorder,
two reels spooling into each other:
my grandfather's voice teaching me
to say my alphabet at age three.
Hearing it, my father stopped
in the hallway, stood in the door,
tilted his head.

I know that look now.
He was running the voice
through the fine comb
of intervening years.
When he turned and went on—
what he wanted to hear
wasn't there.

Simon Bradstreet must have shut that book
once a year on some winter day,
wishing she'd lived just one more week,
until he'd thought to tell her
the right things to say.

Cake

Here's the thing. For two days now
my mind has nibbled at the sweet edge

of future loss, taken little tastes
of a sadness

like icing from the birthday cakes
my mother bought at Alleva's Bakery.

Thick white circles with pink roses
and piping— Happy Birthday in yellow

fancy lettering. I couldn't resist.
I'd run my finger so lightly

over the hard iced ridges,
only at the bottom, on the back,

barely enough to taste, enough
almost to hide.

After dinner, after lighting little candles
and singing, I'd get a whole piece.

But found (I'm sure you guessed)
the stolen delicacy is always more sweet,

lightly touching
leaving the thing so nearly

whole

almost like no day at all
had passed.

III. Casidas

Casida of Waking

Where you are
day is breaking
over the polished leaves
of the orange grove.
Here, the mist
crowds in from the bay
and the small tap
of rain makes me sleepy.
We have lived
half a day apart
for ten years.

When the mist retreats
I will again whisper
a word in its mouth,
a word to carry to you
and you will know
I am the strange tongue
that haunts your dreams,
and your dreams resound
with sitcoms
and miniature golf.
As mine still swirl
in skirts of fire,
mine are full
of stomping feet
and the smell of churros
simmering in open vats of oil,
and the starred and wounded heart
of the Guadalquivir.

Casida of an American Woman

In my bath tonight
I will scrape off the forests of flotilla,
the blonde baby hairs that separate me
from Betty Grable or my grandmother,
women whose calves were smooth as bone,
white and utterly smooth like horn
or china. When my grandmother was laid in
with difficult babies, nurses flocked to her bed
from every floor to look at her legs,
starched hats curving like her ankles,
uniforms white as the underside of her knee.
My grandmother was dainty as a bride doll,
smooth and carefully bred as a nectarine.
The razor glides toward my knee.
I free myself of the wild grass
that weighs me to the earth.
I will be perfect, smooth
as any foreign car
and so American.

Casida of the Lover's Seasons

At the airport you
held me,
said in my ear
"Vente en la primavera."
Come back in the spring.
August bakes and cracks
the plain.
The sparrows gather
on the sill
and suddenly go.
Snows in the Sierra Morenas
close the roads.
In the barrio,
the orange trees bloom
and fail, ten times.
I have come back
ten times
too late.

Casida of the Lover Looking Beyond New Jersey

I live in a city whose name
you never imagined.
I walk between the shadow of dogwood
and the shadow of elm,
eight years from the olive grove
where I held your wrist,
crying, fingers pleading with
the secret skin
behind your elbow.

By the Delaware Bay,
that estuarine lap of ocean,
where she carries her children,
where the rollers plead like fingers,
smoothing and stirring the curved beach,
where blue crab and mussel
flicker in the furrows,
I sit,

gazing past that sandy strip,
that unremarkable garden of New Jersey,
gazing to where, on this same imaginary line,
this convenient curve charted for explorers,
you are walking through the arch of Elvira.

Casida of the Longed-For Lover Forlorn in the Airport

I see your eyes' imprint
burned on the foreheads of my countrymen
who pour from the planes, rush
through terminals.
You are searching; you see my face
in theirs and burn.

You handled their lace fans,
touched the gypsy doll's dress,
played the painted castenets
that say "Recuerdo de Sevilla."

You visit all the tourist shops
on Calle Sierpes and fill them
with your scent— these weightless
reminiscences
passing me in suitcases are drenched in it.
I breathe your breath.

And I am jealous of the gypsy doll!
My skin imagines your hands.
I hear your voice in grocery stores,
luncheon counters. Frustrated,
you're giving words of love
to mushroom pickers, T.V. evangelists,
idle tourists, and, though I've forgotten
the language, forgotten every word you said,
like a dog, like an infant child,
I understand.

Casida of Bible Belt Radio

I'm searching for a human voice
to lament "In My Solitude" with.
But south of the Canal tonight
every other station sells
my personal savior.
They circle my car,
those voices,
swooping,
taloned and sure
while I crawl like a grain mouse
between stubble fields
of sorghum and corn.
I spin the dial
and the fields are full
of static,
the stubble corn
itself singing
in its grave.

IV. The Good Book

Sonny

(the man at my door
speaks of the former tenant
he's come looking for)

"Sonny, well, he just walked in my store and
took
that vacuum cleaner,
told my wife it was for the church
and I'd said o.k.
But I never had,
never had heard of it.
I'm a Christian man
so I don't mind tithin' but I like
to be asked.
I pay my bills,
the Good Book says it,
and he's a minister
and ought to know.
"Render onto Caesar,"
says it right out.
And here he's left me high and dry
and Bobby at the hardware too,
takin' things for the church
and tellin' our wives
when the Bible tells about that too,
dealin' with people's wives and such,
and he should know it.
Skipped out on his rent
in this place and the last one
and ever'day of his life tellin'
how he's about to get some money—
the faithful rich dyin' and leavin'
him cash and then he's gone

again and back with another story,
they ain't none of them true.
Tell the truth the Good Book says,
thou shal't not lie
and Sonny ought to know it
bein' every Sunday
he's standin' in the pulpit.
And the last time I told him
he started in on some truck
about lilies and sewin'."

Adulteress

The first stone struck below my right breast.
I heard the pop and crack
like breaking branches.
The next one bounced from my outstretched
hand and fell heavy to the dust,
uncaught, gray, and even.

They were two or three standing at my door
when I came out to ask them in.
But then the crowd blew up like a whirlwind,
twisting, like the wind through the desert,
rushing, gathering stones and sand.
And I stepped against the sun-warm wall
to find that wind hard and hot
and full of hail.
Hard and hot with stones sent for
my face, my breasts, my arms, my belly,
sent like labor's sudden pain into my belly.

I looked down and saw them in the dust
lying beneath me, mute and gray,
and I fell to my knees and then lay still,
gathering the stone children to me.

Curse of Queen Vashti

When I left Susa,
I did not shake its dust from my feet.
I kept its dust, Ahasuerus, and dragged it
into the desert. I kept its skyline
etched on my eyes.
That city, cursed,
accursed man, Ahasuerus,
to have taken a Jewess to wife
merely because I did not come to heel
like a mongrel bitch.

But the red ants in the desert
reared up on their hind legs
and spoke my name—
and I was changed.
I have eaten desert winds,
writhed with the deadly snake
as he writhed over my bare skin.
I am not dying.
My hair brushes my calves
and I wander in the burning
noon without thirst
and what I have seen
none of your counselors imagine.

Your suns will fall and burst
and burn your buildings, your bright work.
Bright water will be snakebite
and your children will choke.
Faceless beasts will hunt
who walk on their knees
spitting stones and fire.
Then, worst,

your race and hers,
your children for generations
stretching into time like ripples
in this desert, they will burn,
their skin crackling like old paper,
their eyes like brown leaves,
sweet tongues like charred meat,
consumed,
in the hot grip
of your marriage bed.

Crickets

We poked butter knives under the wainscoting,
coaxing crickets into the air,
caught them under cups.
Because someone told me killing them
was bad luck, we planned
to catch them all
and let them go.

So we ran, bent low
and laughing as they arched
beautifully away. Eight of us,
scattered now, lived
together in that summer house
where white cups sprouted
like mushrooms
and each cup housed a bright voice.

Voice on a Train Out of Grand Central

I was a coke addict but I'm clean now.
I come from an addicted family. My mother
was an alcoholic. But when she sobered up I
     figured
I had to. She's 71. I see her on T.V. doing
     commercials
for that rehab out on Montauk, near my house.
     My house
overlooks the Sound. Well, my husband's
     house.
My husband's paintings. My husband's
     Porsche. He
was angry that I let the boy drive it— more
     angry
about the Porsche than that I slept with the
     boy. Well, I say
"boy." He was 24. He could have had any
     young thing he wanted
but he picked me. He didn't mind that I'm fat.
He used to make me look into mirrors, wanted
     me to look at myself
while we were doing it. I hated that. I'm 47.
     Really. But I don't
feel guilty. You know once every six months
     isn't enough for me. Do you
know my husband never put his tongue in my
     mouth? Never. Can you imagine?
No wonder I went crazy with this 24 year old!
     Until his mother broke it up—
I called her a Nazi bitch. She's German. I said
     it to her.
What do I care what she thinks. She's got his

balls in her purse, that's what.
I gave him things. You know, little bribes,
the whole older-woman-younger-man game.
I don't think he would have gone out with me
        if I didn't have the Porsche.
Of course the Porsche is my husband's. My
        husband gets up
early every morning and takes it and I can't
get myself out of bed. My husband's got so
        much energy.
He makes banjoes, has his Ph.D. in
        psychology. He has amazing
self-control. He can make a gram of coke last
        for months. If it were me
I'd do it all up as fast as I could and it would
        be gone. That's why
he can do it and I can't. But he's so tight
        assed! When we have sex
he's got to have the movies and I have to be on
        top.
It's all so structured. My therapist says
        subliminate,
says invest in vibrators, but I want my
        husband.
So maybe I'll come on to the therapist. He's so
cute and I heard a rumor his wife had an affair.
But he'd probably say the rapport
had been broken. He'd send me to somebody
        else.
See those? They're grebes— brown diving
        ducks.
I don't go to church anymore but sometimes
        when I see
the birds on the Sound I can believe in some
        God for awhile.

Strength

"Our finest traits are treacherous.
Think of Hamlet or Oedipus."
                (This I profess to my
                drama class
                who play their roles row
                by row.)
"We only know
what worked before—
puzzle solvers, pensive doubters—
we all forget the new,
the now might make
our forte fault."

                I say this to them
                like I know, or, more,
                like knowing might
                transform tragedies.

When I saw my father that last Thursday
I could see how sick he was.

                But my role was cast, his
                sunny daughter, so
                I mentioned doctors half-
                heartedly.

"For a stomach ache?" One summer
he drove 200 miles with a broken leg.
Ulcers, pneumonia, nothing could bend
him. His strength— stoic refusal
                (or acceptance maybe.)

                My strength—

congeniality.
I turned to happy topics,
brought up doctors just once more,
         an aside, half in jest
         as it were, and when he
         laughed

         and denied again the need
         for one,
I laughed along— my comic role.
                    And let it go.

A Story I Have For Parties

Tressa Repice *did* sit up front
in sixth period History of the Bible.
This small round woman,
Sister Mary of the Rosary
(we called her Beads), preached
that only a hardcover book made
a man's lap a safe seat; paperback
does not do.
She tongue-lashed Tressa repeatedly
for her unchaste polish, every nail
a different shade
from merest mauve to wicked wine,
for her uniform-hemmed-to-mid-thigh,
and for her vowels,
not polished pearls, but steamrolled
flat, vowels that smacked
of South Philly.

Beads was explaining, one autumn afternoon,
that Moses' basket never floated through the
        bullrushes.
David's slingshot had not slain Goliath.
Noah's two-by-two and 60 cubits were not
the literal facts. "The Jews created histories,
great pasts
for their great leaders." At this, Beads looked
out
at our rows of maroon uniforms, pulled at her
        crucifix
and said, "Like Joshua stopping the sun, like
        Shadrach,
Meshach and Abednego in the furnace, like . . .
        like . . ."

65

Tressa's hand, that unchaste pallet,
rose to where that hesitation hovered
like the sun above her head.
"Sistah," she called,
"Sistah . . . like, ya mean a virgin birth?"

Well,
that's the way I tell it.
But in fact,
I sat behind Tressa while she
picked at one nail
and stared at the clock.
She never said a word.
Not in class anyway, and not
to me— except once,
waiting for the afternoon bus,
she called me "Drusilla,"
South Philly for "monstrous toad."

And though I often spoke in class,
I tried to answer right.
I tried to be a "bright girl"
and never had the chutzpah
to raise my hand and venture:
"Sister, could it be? Sister, do you mean?"
So later, when I wish I'd said it,
I edit. I revise. The heresy sounds
less heretical in her mouth,
looks less frightening in my eyes,
and in the story I have for parties,
Tressa gets all the laughs.

I'm The Director

This is my fall piece.
It's a smash— full of poignant
regret. I call it
"The Day We Never Had."
Background music— Vivaldi, of course.
Give me a clear fall
morning. Mother and Daughter
driving the expectable winding
wooded roads. Mother touched
with gray. Daughter in her
twenties, smiling. Cut
to Mother waiting
on a bench.
She's taking Daughter
to lunch.
She waits in the stately collegiate
setting, under stately collegiate plaques
bearing names of children killed
in combat since the school began.
Daughter comes
and they walk off together
under golden elms.

That one brings the house down.
But there's another script.
Mother and Daughter walk through crowds
of coeds. Mother tugs her jacket
over her considerable width.
Daughter chats too brightly,
crunching the brittle leaves
with confidence. They eat
somewhere Mother can get a drink,
a dark room where red

candle globes flicker in the afternoon.
Mother begins to slur. Daughter
eats sharply, each bite clicking
the fork against her teeth.

Another scene— passion,
anger, drama.
The real one doesn't play well.
All silence, Mother and Daughter
drive along. Mother searching
for something on the radio.
Shadows, sunlight flow across them,
as if they are submerged.
When Mother drops her off and asks,
Daughter says,
"No, I don't have time
today for lunch." Mother hunches over
the steering wheel to see
her face. But Daughter
is already moving away,
waves without turning.

What does Mother think
driving back through
those beautifully dying forests?
What does she think
driving toward nothing
that needed her,
no one waiting?
I want to know. I
need to know to end
my dramas.
This part's a blank.

Aunt Kate

Maybe she was bright and bored,
or reckless,
or wild,
or love, love was
a possibility.
But whichever Kate
was passed down
through the family,
through the women
as the tongue and soul
of fire. Our curry
pepper, our copper-headed
Kate, who could and did
escape, or outlive,
or assert and refuse
to accept.
And Kate,
big with child
before she had been
locked in wed,
my mother's mother
and her mother said,
sashayed in a skirt
on sunny days
without any slip,
and the boys watched
her legs and the swing
of her widening hips.

And maybe she was angry
that he never came to call,
or was joking, or mad,
or still perhaps that possibility.

But, whichever, Kate,
our story says, two years
of sunny Saturdays later
took Lizzie to St. Joan of Arc's
and sat in back.

And when he walked
down the aisle,
black and white,
flowered lapel,
him,
with his new bride
and his old smile—
our curry pepper
our spit and fire
our Kate
picked up Lizzie
and said
in a voice that
woke the family dead—
"Look, Baby,
there he is. See?
That right there's your Daddy."

A Toast

When she was married, her father bought
      barrel
after barrel of the best made bootleg liquor.
It was 1929, a year before the final quarrel,
and he and Uncle Ed, they didn't speak again,
      were never drunker.
They stayed drunk, singing and sleeping by
      turns,
for nearly ten days after. And she married the
      man, though she swore
never, said he was too short, too bald. Her
      mother said better than to burn
according to Saint Paul, but on the day she
      wore
the white dress and the borrowed blue bow,
      she was not at all sure.
Not at all sure, but the gifts kept coming to
      clutter and roost,
a chafing dish, carving knives, white sheets,
      twelve more
bath towels, enough for all their lives, and
      when they made the toast,
her uncle and her father arm in arm, said
      here's to your life,
(that hand real on her gartered thigh) your life,
      for you can wish for
no better thing than to be a wife.

V. Silent and Infinite Force

The Virgin and the Dynamo

"Before the end, one began to pray to it;
inherited instinct taught the national
expression of man before silent and infinite
force." *The Education of Henry Adams*

St. Teresa of Avila stirring
the soup or scrubbing
stone floors, meditating
on the miracles of the Virgin,
would suddenly rise above
her chores, her levitation
a sign to all
the silent nuns who looked up
astonished at the soles
of her feet, who blessed
themselves quickly
and prayed.
As she prayed
who hovered above them,
prayed fervently to be
put back down,
                    prayed
as she watched the soup boil,
watched her soapy water
cool on dirty stones.

When he sat in the plush seat of the Ferris
Wheel,
having paid his fifty cents,
the longest piece of steel ever forged,
forty-five feet, lifted him over the fairgrounds.
Chicago 1893, below his swinging soles
the White City sparkled, teamed

75

with machines.
In the midway, "Little Egypt"
danced the hootchy-cootchy.
A tall Arabian swallowed
thin swords.
The first zipper, Cream of Wheat,
rickshaws, fur-bearing trout,
these thrilled the crowds.
From above Henry Adams watched
as it grew smaller and smaller
speeding off
then large again on his return.

And he learned,
like Teresa before,
he found the vision has a price.
The force you feel
will lift you up.
The force you pray to
will let you down
in the landscape of your loss
where by now
you don't belong.

The Discourse of Light: New York World's Fair Grounds
Juniata Park

I. Hall of Science (1990)

We spent hours there one day
calling each other from deception
to deception, each trick
opening before our eyes
their own dark chasms.

We stared into a lens watching
our own rhythmic capillaries.
We stepped into the mirror box
and saw an infinite number
of us, some laughing, some
turned away.

Then, sitting, separated from you
by a desk and glass pane,
I flashed the light on my side
until half the pane was mirror,
until I saw half my face
bearded and smiling,
half yours graced with my eye,
my earring.

Like that freak show act,
or Plato's hypothesis, we were one—
imperfectly matched—
whole an instant in the flash.

II. Unisphere (1963)

The early model Polaroid, a wedding gift,
if they'd put it in the hands of some passerby
and said, "Please?" the light could lift
that image, bring it to my eyes, here,
thirty years away.

Two in the center,
The crowd milling behind.
All swimming in spring light;
all intent on miracles:
glass elevators, lasers, loud
music pumped in
from exotic lands. In each stall,
a treasure. The wedding ring
strange on her finger,
still no well-worn groove.

Before the bloody lips, the drinking,
the specialists, when the hands
were freshly sworn. They might
have stood before the Unisphere;
in that picture they might
almost have born it
on their shoulders,
that huge empty earth.

Cattle Egret

The egret steps
decorously
beyond the clumsy
hoof's indifferent threat,
but stretches
back its long
apology, beak and neck,
to feed on
the ruminating force
that tolerates it.

Jumping Jacks

Windshield wipers
battling November rain
could almost sweep
the night clear, find Venus
suspended from a quarter moon,
find the stars
executing their slow leap into dawn.

All sweeping motions, however mundane,
retain drama.
Our bodies' symmetries mean
synchronous leaps to connection:
the powerful sweep of the dancer,
limbs journeying out and back,
or even my father demonstrating
the jumping jack.

In truth, it's not to Graham or Barishnikov
my mind jumps,
but to my father in sunny suburbia,
furniture pushed against the walls
holding up the US Army Physical Training
Manual.

A private at attention, arms at his side,
then legs wide arms overhead.
He is flanked
by arrows to show his progress (or lack)
as though he has wings, or
has made snow angels
on the perfectly white backdrop.

My father got the book in Basic,
no doubt. Then went AWOL
and came home, scot-free,
threatening the sergeant
that fire burns paper and the records
the Army couldn't replace
and the accounts the sergeant didn't know
could be undone
by one arch of the match.

Then my father flew back
to sweep my mother off her feet
(or so she said after)
and her belly rose like a loaf of bread.
She bore each of us, one after the other,
until four leapt around him,
laughing, out of rhythm, out of breath.

There is nothing as impossible as
teaching children the simple grace
of jumping jacks. Going away
can be one motion with coming back.

"Like scissors," you said, "like wings,"
and we tried to learn the drama
of your sweeping arms, your going out,
your coming home.

Improvising on the Lute

I know what it must be to sleep with you,
to turn in your lap
as the curved lute turns,
round bottomed, smoothed
between your thighs. You finger the spaces
out of sleep, open. What you make curving
one into the other, deeply separate together,
grows, perishable and insistent,
as a child.

Field

Going North on 72, going off
into the forests and foothills
of Pennsylvania, I know
a field. Its grasses are
hip-deep and brown in October,
its rise and fall, breathing,
its quick curves are yours.

Some evening this autumn
I will crawl into the center
and fall asleep.
My hands will be
the wind in the grass.

Processional

The river rides under the traffic bridges,
under the derricks and the telephone wires.
The river turns below Martin Luther King
   Boulevard,
below the boarded windows of Berger Brothers
Office Furniture. The river gives back the
   colors
of scrub pine, tarred pile-ons, and early
   summer maple,
gives back the impasto sky.
Beside the river, from this four-story height,
the headlights coming North on I-95 pay
   themselves out
like a rope of shining water from a pump,
not ponderous as the river, but quick,
like cold water pouring into the June dusk of
   Wilmington.
The river is rising in the name of the tides,
and the moon, and the rainy weekend.
No point in its eternity can happen again, as
   Heraclites
said, speaking of his own veins growing old,
his own light, paying itself out like a rope of
   bright water.

Anne Colwell, a poet and fiction writer, is an Associate Professor of English at the University of Delaware. Her work has appeared in several journals, including: *California Quarterly, Mudlark, Evansville Review, Eclectic Literary Forum, Southern Poetry Review, Stickman Review, Poetry Bay,* and *Octavo.* An online chapbook of her poems appears in *The Alsop Review.* Her critical book, *Inscrutable Houses: Metaphors of the Body in the Poems of Elizabeth Bishop,* was published by the University of Alabama Press in 1997. She received an Established Artist Award in Poetry and an Emerging Artist Award in Fiction from the Delaware State Arts Council. She lives in Milton, Delaware with her husband James Keegan and son, Thomas.

LaVergne, TN USA
22 September 2010
198018LV00001B/9/P